Saint Gianna Beretta Molla

Saint Gianna Beretta Molla
The Gift of Life

Written by
Susan Helen Wallace, FSP
with
Patricia Edward Jablonski, FSP

Illustrated by Rick Powell

BOOKS & MEDIA
Boston

Library of Congress Cataloging-in-Publication Data

Wallace, Susan Helen, 1940-

  Saint Gianna Beretta Molla : the gift of life / written by Susan Helen Wallace with Patricia Edward Jablonski ; illustrated by Rick Powell.

   p. cm. -- (Encounter the saints series)

   ISBN-13: 978-0-8198-7182-4

   ISBN-10: 0-8198-7182-6

 1. Beretta Molla, Gianna, Saint, 1922-1962--Juvenile literature. 2. Christian saints--Italy--Biography--Juvenile literature. I. Jablonski, Patricia E. II. Powell, Rick, 1963- III. Title.

   BX4700.B42W35 2012

   282.092--dc23

   [B]

                                    2011038642

Cover art/Illustrated by Rick Powell

All rights reserved. No part of this book may be reproduced or transmitted in any form or by any means, electronic or mechanical, including photocopying, recording, or by any information storage and retrieval system, without permission in writing from the publisher.

"P" and PAULINE are registered trademarks of the Daughters of Saint Paul.

Copyright © 2012, Daughters of Saint Paul

Published by Pauline Books & Media, 50 Saint Pauls Avenue, Boston, MA 02130-3491

Printed in the U.S.A.

SBBMVSA USA PEOILL12-1J11-09151 7182-6

www.pauline.org

Pauline Books & Media is the publishing house of the Daughters of Saint Paul, an international congregation of women religious serving the Church with the communications media.

1 2 3 4 5 6 7 8 9   15 14 13 12

Encounter the Saints Series

Blesseds Jacinta and Francisco Marto
Shepherds of Fatima

Blessed John Paul II
Be Not Afraid

Blessed Pier Giorgio Frassati
Journey to the Summit

Blessed Teresa of Calcutta
Missionary of Charity

Journeys with Mary
Apparitions of Our Lady

Saint André Bessette
Miracles in Montreal

Saint Anthony of Padua
Fire and Light

Saint Bakhita of Sudan
Forever Free

Saint Bernadette Soubirous
And Our Lady of Lourdes

Saint Clare of Assisi
A Light for the World

Saint Damien of Molokai
Hero of Hawaii

Saint Edith Stein
Blessed by the Cross

Saint Elizabeth Ann Seton
Daughter of America

Saint Faustina Kowalska
Messenger of Mercy

Saint Frances Xavier Cabrini
Cecchina's Dream

Saint Francis of Assisi
Gentle Revolutionary

Saint Gianna Beretta Molla
The Gift of Life

Saint Ignatius of Loyola
For the Greater Glory of God

Saint Isaac Jogues
With Burning Heart

Saint Joan of Arc
God's Soldier

Saint John Vianney
A Priest for All People

Saint Juan Diego
And Our Lady of Guadalupe

Saint Katharine Drexel
The Total Gift

Saint Martin de Porres
Humble Healer

Saint Maximilian Kolbe
Mary's Knight

Saint Paul
The Thirteenth Apostle

Saint Pio of Pietrelcina
Rich in Love

Saint Teresa of Avila
Joyful in the Lord

Saint Thérèse of Lisieux
The Way of Love

*To my mother, Helen,
who loved being a mother
as did Saint Gianna*

Contents

1. Memories 1
2. Gift Number Ten 5
3. Jesus Comes 10
4. In Joy, In Sorrow 16
5. The Greatest Journey 19
6. War's Shadow 23
7. Crosses, Blessings, Decisions 28
8. God's Plan 33
9. A Ring for Gianna 37
10. Mrs. Molla 43
11. A Wonderful Surprise 48
12. The First "Treasures" Arrive! 54
13. Life Is Beautiful 60
14. A Time for Joy 64
15. The Way of the Cross 68
16. Good Friday 73

17. Going Home 80

18. Loved Forever 85

19. Pro-Life Saint 90

Prayer 96

Glossary 97

1
MEMORIES

Eleven-year-old Gianna sat at the dining room table surrounded by stacks of photo albums. "There are a lot of people in these pictures, and I don't even know who some of them are!" she exclaimed.

"Like who?" asked her older sister, Amalia, as she walked by carrying a pile of folded laundry.

"Like this cute little boy," Gianna responded, pointing to an old black and white photograph.

Amalia set down the clothes and stopped to have a look. "That's Papa, silly!" she chuckled. Slipping the picture out of the album, she turned it over. "See, it's written here on the back: 'Alberto Beretta at age four.' This photograph must have been taken not long after our grandmother died," Amalia continued. "See, his eyes look sad."

"Sad?" Gianna asked thoughtfully. "What else can you tell me about Papa and Mama?" Gianna prodded. "I don't think they have time to answer all the questions I'd like to ask, and you know so many things that I've never heard about before."

"It's just because I'm twice your age," Amalia answered with a grin.

Amalia pulled out a chair and sat down. "Well, several years after his mama died, Papa was sent away from his hometown of Magenta, to live at a Catholic boarding school in Milan. Papa was a good student and got along well with everyone, but he really missed his family at home. He was very lonely."

"Maybe that's why family is so important to Papa," Gianna observed.

"I'm sure it is," Amalia agreed. "Now to get back to what I was saying. When Papa was in his twenties, he met the young woman he knew he wanted to marry—Maria De Micheli."

"It was Mama, right?" Gianna interrupted.

"Right," nodded Amalia. "She was six years younger than Papa, but their friendship was a perfect fit, and soon they were planning their wedding!"

"Mama was the oldest in her family, wasn't she?"

"Yes, she was. And being the oldest of five girls, she had had plenty of opportunity to help her mother take care of her younger sisters. This experience prepared her to start her own family—our family."

The parlor clock suddenly chimed the hour. "I didn't realize it was so late!" Gianna exclaimed. "I'd better get all this put away. It's almost time for dinner. Thanks for filling me in on some of our family history, Amalia."

"It was fun," Amalia answered. "Let's look through old photos again some time. Who knows what treasures we'll find!"

Alberto and Maria had married on October 12, 1908. They certainly couldn't afford a honeymoon, but they were happy just the same. They began their married life in the city of Milan, not far from a large Capuchin Franciscan monastery. The newlyweds closed their apartment door behind them and smiled. "It's not much," Alberto apologized. "I wish I could give you more, Maria."

"What are you talking about?" his young wife countered. "It's beautiful, Alberto . . . and it's our very own. Here we'll begin a whole new life!"

"This is just what I've always dreamed of," Alberto confided, "a family of my own. And you are the only woman I have ever wanted to be my wife." Maria blushed and hugged her husband. Alberto noticed that her eyes were bright with tears.

The ordinary pace of life began right away. Alberto went daily to his job at the Cantoni Cotton Mill, while Maria busied herself with transforming their little apartment into a cozy home.

Twenty years and thirteen children later, Alberto and Maria Beretta had experienced joys and heartaches in their life together. Three of their children—David, Rosina, and Pierina—had died of the dreaded Spanish flu. The terrible epidemic broke out in 1918. It has been estimated that it claimed between fifty and one hundred million victims worldwide, far more than the fifteen million people who died in World War I.

Two more of the couple's children, Guglielmina and Anna Maria, died as infants. The eight Beretta children who grew to adulthood were Amalia, Francesco, Ferdinando, Enrico, Zita, Giuseppe, Gianna, and Virginia.

Alberto and Maria never dreamed that someday one of their children would be canonized a saint. But, that's exactly what happened. The story begins with Gianna's birth.

2
Gift Number Ten

Alberto paced back and forth, anxiously awaiting news. In the 1920s, most children were born at home, and on the other side of the bedroom door Maria was now giving birth to their tenth child. It was the feast of St. Francis of Assisi, Wednesday, October 4, 1922. *Each child born into the world is a precious gift from God,* Alberto thought. *And it's an added gift from St. Francis to have our newest child born on his feast day!* Alberto and Maria were members of the Third Order of St. Francis and had a special love for their patron saint.

Soon, a newborn's cry echoed through the house. The bedroom door swung open. "Come in, Mr. Beretta," waved the midwife. "Come and see your beautiful little girl!"

One week later, on October 11, the infant, dressed in a delicate white baptismal gown and a ruffled, close-fitting cap, was brought to the Basilica of St. Martin in the city of Magenta. Wide-eyed, she looked up at the smiling faces surrounding her. "What's she thinking?" her brothers and sisters asked each other as they vied for her attention. The priest carefully poured water over the little girl's head as he pronounced the sacramental words: "I baptize you Giovanna Francesca, in the name of the Father, and of the Son, and of the Holy Spirit. Amen."

Giovanna Francesca returned home that day a child of God and a new member of the Catholic Church. It wasn't long before her parents and family began calling her "Gianna."

The Beretta family lived in times of upheaval. World War I had deeply affected Italy and all of Europe in many ways. In the years immediately following the war, peace remained a very cautious hope.

Mr. and Mrs. Beretta often talked about the world situation. After having already lost three children, the safety and happiness of the rest of their family was their highest priority.

"Maria, I was thinking that it would be better if we could move further away from Milan to a place in the countryside," Alberto said one evening as his wife poured him a cup of coffee. "Perhaps Bergamo—the air is cleaner because of the high altitude and the children will be healthier and safer there. That would be a plus for Amalia, with those weak lungs of hers. Maybe she wouldn't get sick so often."

Maria frowned. "Alberto," she quietly replied, "think of all the time you'll lose traveling every day. It's a distance of fifty-eight kilometers (thirty-six miles) each way..."

"I know Bergamo is farther from my job at the factory, but I could always take a train," Alberto broke in. "Don't forget, I'll still be home on Sundays."

Maria gave her husband a quick hug. "All right. I agree, if you think it's for the best."

"I do, Maria. I really do," he answered.

Mr. Beretta wasted no time in traveling to Bergamo to find a large enough home that they could afford. He was successful. Best of all, the house had a garden where the children could enjoy the outdoors. The family was even more excited, because Maria's parents lived nearby.

The Berettas soon settled into their new home, and Mr. Beretta began his new and unfamiliar daily routine. He started his day in the parish church with 5:00 AM Mass, then took the train to his job at the factory in Milan.

At that time, the eucharistic fast in preparation for receiving Holy Communion began the previous midnight. That meant that Mr. Beretta and the other worshippers did not eat breakfast before attending the early morning Mass. Because he had had no food or water since midnight the night before, when Alberto boarded the train to go to work, he was hungry!

As the train rattled along, Mr. Beretta would open his lunch box and snack on some fresh fruit and a piece of his wife's homemade bread. And always he would offer a prayer of thanks for God's many blessings. Alberto had to admit that he was a happy man. "God has given me everything I have asked for," he whispered to himself, "and the greatest gift is my family."

Gianna was only three when her family moved to Bergamo. For her, it was a real adventure! How happy she was when the family gathered each evening after supper to listen to the beautiful music her sister

Amalia played on the piano. Then came family prayer time. Before a large picture of the Sacred Heart and a statue of the Blessed Mother, the Berettas would pray the Rosary. Gianna watched and listened from her safe perch on her mother's lap. Although she was too young to understand all that was going on, she knew that it was special. She felt loved—by her family, and by God.

3
JESUS COMES

"Mama wants me to begin preparing you for your first Holy Communion," Amalia announced one day with a warm smile. "What do you think about that?"

Gianna's eyes lit up. "I can hardly wait!" the five-year-old exclaimed, her round face flushing with excitement. Brushing her dark bangs from her forehead, the little girl was ready to get down to business. "When can we start?"

"Right now!" Amalia replied, opening up a catechism.

Amalia began to tell Gianna all about the Eucharist, and how receiving Holy Communion was really receiving a special visit from Jesus.

"I like the way you tell stories and answer all my questions," Gianna complimented her sister at the end of the lesson. "You're a good teacher!"

"Well," Amalia grinned, "I'm glad you approve of me."

It was fun having Amalia all to herself every day for a private lesson. Gianna enjoyed the six months she spent learning more about her Catholic faith from her eldest sixteen-year-old sister. Toward the end of her preparation time, though, Gianna had a special request. "Amalia, can we go down to the church for a Communion class? I want to ask you about the altar and the tiny house that Jesus lives in. And I want to know how the little white hosts are made. And please tell me about the Stations of the Cross and all the statues, especially the one of Mother Mary."

"Yes, we can go to the church and talk about all of that," Amalia agreed. "I'll teach you how to go to Penance, too."

Gianna was becoming more and more excited about receiving her first Holy Communion. Although she was only five-and-a-half-years old, she was included in that year's first Communion class. "I believe that your little student is ready to receive Jesus in the Eucharist," the pastor had confided to Amalia. "I have no doubts that she understands what a great gift the Eucharist is. You've done an excellent job instructing her, Amalia."

At last the big day, Saturday, April 14, 1928, arrived. The whole Beretta family gathered for the happy occasion. Gianna

Jesus comes to Gianna.

looked radiant in her lovely white dress. A little cross hung from a golden chain around her neck. Wearing a long veil capped by a crown of white flowers, she knelt at the altar rail to receive Jesus for the very first time. Gianna spoke heart to heart with the Lord. There were so many things she wanted to tell him—most especially that she loved him.

After Mass, Gianna's family had a photograph taken as a special keepsake. The little girl, her dark eyes flashing, stared somberly into the camera. She held her new white prayer book and rosary solemnly in her left hand. Gianna was told to look serious and prayerful about receiving Jesus into her heart. *Maybe I should have smiled at the camera to show how happy I really am,* she thought afterward. *But that's all right. Jesus knows everything. He came to visit me, and he will come again. Now we're very close!*

After her first Holy Communion, Gianna accompanied her mother, brothers, and sisters every morning to Mass. Jesus was now alive in Gianna's heart even more fully. She was beginning to think, act, and love more and more like him, and making sacrifices didn't seem to bother her. Sunny days, rainy days, cold days—the weather never stopped the Beretta family. Jesus came first. From the time she was a young child, Gianna attended Mass and received Communion nearly every day for the rest of her life.

Two years later on June 8, 1930, seven-year-old Gianna received the sacrament of Confirmation at the Cathedral of Bergamo. At that time, it was not unusual for children to be confirmed at a young age. The Cathedral of Saint Alexander was very special to the Catholics of Bergamo because it was dedicated to the patron of their city. Gianna and the other children who were confirmed that day must have been excited to receive the special coming of the Holy Spirit in such an important church.

Life in the Beretta family continued to be a joyful experience. Maria and Alberto loved to spend time listening to all their children share what they had learned about the world and their Catholic faith in school. The children also understood how important education was to their mother and father.

"We want each of you to live a happy, fulfilled life and make this world a better place," Mr. Beretta explained one evening after the family prayers were over. "We know that a good education costs money—but your Mama and I are willing to work hard to help you. You each have special gifts and talents, and we want you to discover and develop them."

What's my special gift? Gianna began to wonder. *I'm not sure what it is yet, but it's exciting to think about!*

4
IN JOY, IN SORROW

"Gianna and Virginia, both of you, bring me your homework so I can look it over," Mrs. Beretta called.

Mama Beretta took a personal interest in each of her children's schoolwork. She was always there to encourage them in every possible way. In fact, she even learned Latin and Greek to help a few of her struggling language scholars!

Gianna was not one of those children who love school. If she had had her way, she would have been outside playing, listening to music, or painting pictures instead of doing her homework. She especially had trouble with her Italian and Latin classes. Once, she even had to retake the exams in these two subjects in order to pass. Although she wasn't overly enthused about school, Gianna did try her best. She knew that getting a good education would be very important for her future.

Within her warm family circle, Gianna had a special relationship with her youngest sister, Virginia. The two girls, just three years apart, were not only sisters, they were the best of friends. Virginia idolized her big sister. They did practically everything together and trusted each other totally. Virginia especially liked Gianna's way of looking at life with optimism and joy. Speaking about Gianna many years later, Virginia remembered, "Gianna recognized beauty, the way a poet or an artist might. She didn't miss the wonderful things God had made and had shared with his creatures. She especially loved taking trips to the mountains, skiing, literature, art, and music. She was grateful for all of life's good gifts."

In spite of their happy family life, Gianna noticed that her Mama and Papa sometimes looked serious and talked in hushed voices so that the children couldn't hear them. One evening, she walked in on their conversation. "What's wrong, Maria?" she heard her father ask. "You look so worried. I can tell that something is bothering you."

"Yes, Alberto, it is. I've been thinking a lot lately," Mrs. Beretta answered. "We moved here to Bergamo because we hoped it would provide a healthier environment for the children. But, in the twelve years that we've spent here, little Guglielmina and Anna Maria have gone back to God. And have you noticed how pale Amalia looks? She's always coughing . . . Maybe Bergamo wasn't such a good choice after all."

Alberto sighed and tapped his fingers on the armrest of his chair. "If we have to move again for the sake of the children," he said decisively, "we will."

Sadly, Amalia, who had suffered from respiratory disease for many years, died at the age of twenty-six on January 22, 1937. Her death brought great sorrow to the whole family, but especially to Gianna, who was fifteen, and Virginia, who was twelve at the time. Each had treasured memories of their older sister, and both of them missed her terribly. Gianna, deep in thought, reflected on the treasure that Amalia had been to her. She thought back to the time she had spent with her, preparing for her first Holy Communion. "I miss you so much, Amalia," she whispered, "may you be with the Lord and his Mother. Look down on us now and pray for us. Help our family. Help *me*."

5

THE GREATEST JOURNEY

Shortly after Amalia's death, fear of further illness led the Berettas to pack up and move again. Many people believed that it was healthiest to live near the ocean, or in the mountains. This time they settled in Quinto al Mare, a university city not far from Genoa on the Italian Riviera. Mr. Beretta was happy because the whole family could still be together.

In Quinto, fifteen-year-old Gianna attended a Catholic school run by the Sisters of St. Dorothy. As a teenager, Gianna was growing in the spiritual life. She continued going to daily Mass and Holy Communion with her mother. Now and then, Gianna would steal a glance at her mother, who was always deep in prayer. *This is how a true follower of Jesus prays*, Gianna thought. *This is how I want to pray.*

In March 1938 Jesuit Father Michael Avedano preached a three-day retreat at Gianna's school. It was an experience that filled the young girl with a new outpouring of the Holy Spirit and increased her desire for God. In his talks, Father Avedano especially focused on how we can prepare ourselves for heaven by the way we live here on earth. He encouraged the students to take time for personal reflection and prayer.

Gianna, praying before the Blessed Sacrament in the school chapel, opened her notebook. She just had to write her thoughts on this whole spiritual experience. Her pen flew across each empty page, filling it with thoughts she wanted to remember from Father's talks, prayers she especially liked, and her resolutions for the future. "Jesus," she wrote, "I promise to accept everything that you will allow to happen to me. Help me to know your will."

At the conclusion of the retreat, Gianna came to an important realization: to grow close to God the Holy Trinity is actually a life-long journey. *I want so much to continue this journey,* she thought. *I want to live all that I've learned and experienced during these special days of prayer.*

Gianna knew that she was going to need some guidance on her spiritual path. There was just so much more to learn about God and his will for her! She decided to ask Monsignor Mario Righetti, the pastor of her parish church, for help and advice. Monsignor kindly agreed to become her spiritual director. This meant that the priest would hold brief but regular meetings with Gianna, and help lead her to a deeper awareness of how Jesus was living in her and acting through her.

"Gianna," Monsignor Righetti asked at one of their meetings, "would you ever consider taking charge of the youngest girls of Catholic Action?"

Gianna's surprised look quickly changed to one of interest. She was already a junior member of Catholic Action, an organization of laypersons whose purpose was to influence society and culture with gospel values.

"You could be a great help to the girls in our parish group," Monsignor went on. "It would involve helping the girls learn to pray, giving them little talks on different aspects of our Catholic faith, taking them on outings sponsored by the organization, and perhaps a few other things. I realize that it would require a lot of your time, Gianna, but I think you'd enjoy it. And I'm sure the children would love you. Are you interested?"

"Oh yes, Monsignor!" Gianna enthusiastically exclaimed. "When do I start?"

"How about next week?" the priest replied with a smile.

6
WAR'S SHADOW

"Your Gianna is growing into a fine young woman," a neighbor commented to Mrs. Beretta one morning when they met at the market.

"Yes," Maria agreed with pride. "She certainly is."

By sixteen, Gianna had grown taller and more slender. The signature bangs and short haircut she had worn as a young child had disappeared. Her dark wavy hair now fell casually to her shoulders. Gianna had an outgoing personality. Her smile came easily, a sincere, happy smile. It was contagious.

Since the Beretta children were growing older, there was much talk about their plans for the future when they all got together. "Are you still thinking of becoming a doctor and a Franciscan priest?" Francesco asked Enrico.

"Yes, definitely," Enrico replied with a smile.

"Of course, Nando will make a wonderful family doctor once he finishes medical school," Gianna predicted.

"I bet he won't become upset or annoyed like some doctors do when babies and little children cry in their office," Virginia broke in.

"I'm not so sure about that," Giuseppe interjected.

"And what about you, Gianna?" Zita asked. "What would you like to be?"

"I might become a nun," Gianna answered matter-of-factly.

"Really? What kind?" Virginia prodded.

"Oh, I don't know. I'd like to be a missionary some day. But I still have a lot of praying and thinking to do before I make a decision," Gianna replied in a thoughtful tone.

So much was happening in Gianna's life. Besides her schoolwork, she was now very much involved in Catholic Action. Her natural enthusiasm and ready participation in many worthwhile initiatives were wonderful, but Mr. and Mrs. Beretta could see something that Gianna couldn't: she was overdoing things and needed more rest. Her health and resistance were weakening, and she was becoming susceptible to illness.

Antibiotics were not widely available at the time, so it was not uncommon for a simple illness to become something truly serious. The solution her parents came up with was to have Gianna suspend her studies in order to rebuild her strength.

Gianna realized that her parents had her best interests at heart. She also began to understand her need for a more balanced schedule. She peacefully accepted her parents' decision and stayed at home for a year from 1938–1939. During that year, she grew stronger and more prepared to continue on her way once again.

Just a month before Gianna was scheduled to return to school, Germany invaded Poland. Friday, September 1, 1939, was the official beginning of World War II—a day that would change history.

At first, life remained normal in Quinto al Mare. Gianna went back to the school run by the Sisters of Saint Dorothy and picked up where she had left off in her studies. However, the situation in Europe soon worsened. On June 10, 1940, Italy joined the war on the side of Germany. Gianna rushed to her father as soon as he came home from work that day. "Papa, is it true? Are we really at war?" She couldn't hide the tremor in her voice.

"Papa, are we really at war?"

"Yes. I'm afraid it's true, darling," Mr. Beretta quietly replied as he wrapped his arm around her shoulder. "Now is a time for prayer—prayer for Europe and for the whole world."

The Berettas and their neighbors lived in continual fear as World War II raged around them. Then, during the summer of 1941, their worst nightmare came true—Quinto al Mare was bombed. Mrs. Beretta already had a heart condition, and the added stress brought on by the war was especially bad for her. "I'm terrified of these bombs!" she admitted to her family.

"Don't worry, Maria," her husband soothed. "We're going to leave here as soon as possible."

"But where will we go, Papa?" Virginia asked, her eyes wide with fear.

"Stay calm now. I have it all worked out. We'll go to our summer home in the mountains, near Switzerland. Viggiona will be good for now, and in the fall we'll move back to Bergamo, to your grandparents' home."

Mrs. Beretta sighed in relief. "May God protect us all," she whispered. "May God protect us all!"

7

CROSSES, BLESSINGS, DECISIONS

A month after the Berettas had relocated to Bergamo, the bombing in the area had quieted down. Nineteen-year-old Gianna returned as a boarding student to finish school in Quinto al Mare. It was November 1941. She missed her family very much, but her busy academic schedule helped the days to pass quickly. She began each morning, as always, with Mass and Holy Communion.

Although life returned to normal—at least for a while—Gianna and her family were soon called to bear a sorrow even greater than the war: Mrs. Beretta suffered a heart attack and passed into eternal life on April 29, 1942. She was fifty-five. Still recovering from the pain and loss of their mother, Gianna and her brothers and sisters were shaken by the death of their father just four months later on September 10. *Lord,* Gianna prayed, *I don't understand your ways, but I trust you. I know that you love us. I believe that all life is in your hands, and that you allow everything only for our good. Reward Mama and Papa with much peace and joy. Help us imitate the example they left us.*

After the deaths of their parents, Gianna and her siblings decided to return to Magenta, where there were strong family ties and many happy memories. Gianna had graduated from high school that June. Following her brothers Enrico and Ferdinando, Gianna decided to become a doctor and made plans to attend medical school in nearby Milan. No one who knew her was surprised. She had always been a compassionate young woman with a special love for those who were poor and sick.

Gianna began her studies at the Faculty for Medicine and Surgery of the University of Milan in November 1942. It was difficult to continue medical school while all of Europe was at war. Gianna's classes were often cancelled, especially when bombs began to fall on Milan. So, in 1945, she transferred to the University of Pavia, a smaller school in a less important city.

Gianna worked hard to complete all the requirements to become a doctor. She attended classes, spent time in the university laboratory, and learned how to treat patients by working alongside experienced doctors.

On November 30, 1949, twenty-seven-year-old Gianna finally received her medical degree. *My Lord*, the young doctor prayed, *help me to grow in gratitude for all who have enabled me to complete this part of my life's journey. I thank you, dear God, first of all, then Mama, Papa, all my brothers and sisters, relatives, professors, and everyone who helped me along the way. May I always use my knowledge to be an instrument of healing and comfort for others.*

Now that she had her medical degree, Gianna's thoughts turned to her brother, Enrico. He had become a doctor and a Capuchin Franciscan priest, taking the name Father Alberto. Father Alberto had recently been sent to Brazil as a medical missionary. After a lot of prayer, Gianna had realized that God wasn't calling her to become a nun, but reading her brother's letters about his work among the people in Brazil, she began to wonder if she should become a lay missionary and travel there to assist him. *So many sick children there need help,* she reasoned. *I can start to study a little Portuguese now so I'll be ready if Enrico agrees that I should come.*

Gianna decided to confide her desires to her brother Giuseppe, who had been ordained a priest in the Bergamo diocese two years before Enrico's ordination. Father

Giuseppe listened, thought for a few moments, and responded with carefully chosen words. "You're not that strong, Gianna, and the climate and living conditions in Brazil are very different from those here in Italy. You know how much you suffer from the heat, and Brazil is in the tropics. It takes a lot of stamina and physical strength to minister in the missions. You need to really think this over and pray more about it, as your spiritual director has suggested. I'll ask Bishop Bernareggi what he would advise you to do. He's a very wise and prudent person."

The bishop agreed that it wasn't clear that Gianna had been called to a missionary vocation. He suggested that she continue to wait and pray to see where God was leading her. Gianna accepted his advice.

In the meantime, she set to work. In the summer of 1950, she opened an office in the nearby town of Mesero, in the same building where her brother, Dr. Ferdinando Beretta, had his medical practice. There were not very many women doctors at the time, and not everyone was comfortable with the idea of women pursuing a career as a physician. But Gianna had no trouble attracting patients. The kind doctor's days were very full. Every morning she visited patients in their homes or in the hospital. In the afternoons, she saw patients at her office. On top of all this, she also took specialized classes at the University of Milan so that she could become a pediatrician.

For Gianna, practicing medicine was a mission, not just a job. She saw it as her way of living out Jesus's command that we love God by loving one another. As a Christian, she believed that doctors cared for Jesus himself in the bodies of those who were sick. Gianna offered her services to everyone, whether they were able to pay her or not. Sometimes patients who couldn't afford a doctor's care would give Gianna a chicken, or eggs, or a bouquet of flowers. She often gave patients free medicine and even money.

Gianna left her office only after the last patient had been seen—no matter how late or how long her day was. But while she cared for people's bodies, the young doctor was also concerned for their souls. She was known for her goodness and for the way she encouraged the sick. Gianna wanted to lead everyone she met closer to God. *Use me, Jesus, as your instrument for doing good*, she prayed.

8
GOD'S PLAN

"The blood transfusion is over, Teresina," Gianna said softly as she stroked the woman's hand. "How are you feeling?"

"A little better," the twenty-seven-year-old patient answered feebly.

Gianna turned away in order to hide her own sorrow. Teresina was dying of nephritis, a progressive kidney disease. There was nothing more she could do other than keep her comfortable. Just then, a concerned-looking visitor slipped quietly into the hospital room. "I'm her brother," he whispered to Gianna, "Pietro Molla." The doctor nodded and smiled. "Thank you for coming," she whispered back.

Teresina died a few days later. But Pietro never forgot the doctor who had attended her with unusual kindness and concern. Thinking back, he realized that he had actually met Gianna once before. It was at Dr. Ferdinando Beretta's office where he had gone for an appointment. Noticing Pietro gazing at her, one of the waiting patients had remarked in a low voice, "Dr. Ferdinando is fortunate to have such a fine sister, such an approachable and caring young doctor."

Pietro, himself a member of Catholic Action, had also heard of all the good Gianna did in her work for that organization. He had seen her but had not spoken to her when she occasionally visited his parish to speak to the young people. Now it seemed God had a plan to bring Gianna and Pietro together.

It was the feast of the Immaculate Conception, December 8, 1954. Father Lino Garavaglia, a newly ordained Capuchin Franciscan priest was celebrating his first Mass. Among the many guests at the liturgy and reception were Gianna and Pietro. She was the Garavaglia's family doctor. He was their neighbor and a family friend.

After the Mass, the guests moved to a large room decorated for the celebration. Without any pre-planning, Gianna and Pietro ended up sitting right across from each other. Gianna's warm gaze focused on Pietro. *This is the brother of Teresina*, she recalled. *A very thoughtful and quiet man*. Her gentle voice reached out to him from across the table. "Mr. Molla, do you remember our meeting in the hospital when your sister was so ill?"

Pietro smiled and nodded.

"I'm so sorry that there was not more we could have done for her," Gianna continued, "but we have faith that she is with our Lord and isn't suffering anymore."

"Thank you so much, Doctor," Pietro replied. "My family and I truly appreciate all you did for Teresina."

Gianna is so outgoing, Pietro thought to himself. *She makes everyone feel at home. I wish I weren't so shy. I can't think of much to say . . .*

Gianna appeared eager to continue their conversation. "You know that I'm a physician, Mr. Molla, but I was wondering what type of work you do." Her lovely smile seemed to say, "I really am interested, you know!"

"I'm an engineer," Pietro said simply, "a director at the La Saffa factory. We manufacture matches and plastics of all kinds."

Gianna nodded in approval. "I imagine your life is very busy."

"As a matter of fact, it really is," Pietro answered. "I've been working at La Saffa for a long time, and I do a lot of traveling for the company. I'm sent to cities all across Europe and America."

"It must be hard for you to be away from your family so much," the doctor said sympathetically.

"Well . . . actually . . . I'm not married," Pietro confessed. He could feel his face reddening. "Travel is not a problem for me, although I wish I had time to do more with Catholic Action and my parish," Pietro stopped. He hoped that he hadn't sounded as if he were bragging.

Gianna didn't seem to notice. She happily chatted on. Little by little, Pietro began to relax. What became a deep friendship was born that day. The two agreed to see each other again.

"By the way," Pietro said quietly as Gianna rose to leave, "I just have to tell you . . . you really are quite beautiful!"

Gianna smiled graciously. "Why thank you, Mr. Molla."

By now, Pietro's shyness had mostly evaporated. "Please, call me Pietro," he said as he helped Gianna into her coat.

"Why thank you, Pietro," Gianna beamed.

9

A RING FOR GIANNA

Soon Gianna and Pietro began to date. As they shared more and more of their hopes and dreams, Gianna realized that they had a lot in common. After years of praying, discerning, and seeking the advice of her spiritual director, Gianna's questions about her vocation in life were finally resolved. *I'm not called to be a missionary in Brazil*, she realized. *The Lord is asking me to be a good Christian doctor and wife, and if he blesses us with children—a mother. How wonderful that Pietro is the man I will marry!*

Gianna liked to voice the feelings of her heart on paper, and was a dedicated letter writer. "Dearest Pietro," she wrote in her very first letter to him. "I already love you now, and I would like to build a true Christian family with you."

On Easter Monday, April 11, 1955, Gianna and Pietro were officially engaged. Pietro had been so excited that he gave Gianna her engagement ring a few days earlier. Gianna's brother, Father Giuseppe, celebrated a special Mass for the couple, making their engagement day even more of a celebration. The Mass took place in the chapel of the Daughters of Charity of Canossia, the religious congregation that Gianna's younger sister Virginia had entered.

A few months later, on June 10, 1955, Gianna wrote with an open heart, "I love you so much, Pietro, and you are always with me, beginning in the morning with Holy Mass . . ."

The couple's time of engagement was full of joy for Gianna. "I trust in the goodness of God," she said. "He will lead my future husband and me on the path of the vocation we've chosen. We both truly believe that marriage is a vocation. It's a lifetime commitment. We want to walk the path together, sharing in mutual trust."

The date was set for the wedding: Saturday, September 24, 1955. The couple's many conversations and letters centered on marriage, the family they hoped to have, and making plans for a happy life together.

"What can I do to make you *really* happy, Pietro?" Gianna asked one day.

"Just be yourself," Pietro replied with a grin. "Being with you is what makes me happy. Sharing what is important to us brings me joy."

The couple treasured their openness with each other. Gianna confided to Pietro her deep convictions about being a physician. "As a doctor, I know that my patients have souls as well as bodies," she said. "They trust me to respect them and to care for them. It's a real privilege. I'd like to go on practicing medicine even after we're married, Pietro, if you're open to the idea." At that time, married women were usually supported financially by their husbands, and expected to stay home in order to care for their children.

"I know how much being a doctor means to you," Pietro reassured her. "I don't see why you can't keep up your medical practice along with family responsibilities. I know you can do it."

Pietro also loved his job and the company he worked for. But he realized that his work would also present challenges to their married life. Frequent business trips would require him to spend time away from home. Gianna understood. "Don't worry, Pietro," she replied. "With God to help us, everything will work out just fine. We can trust him, you'll see."

As the countdown to the wedding date continued, Gianna worked harder than ever.

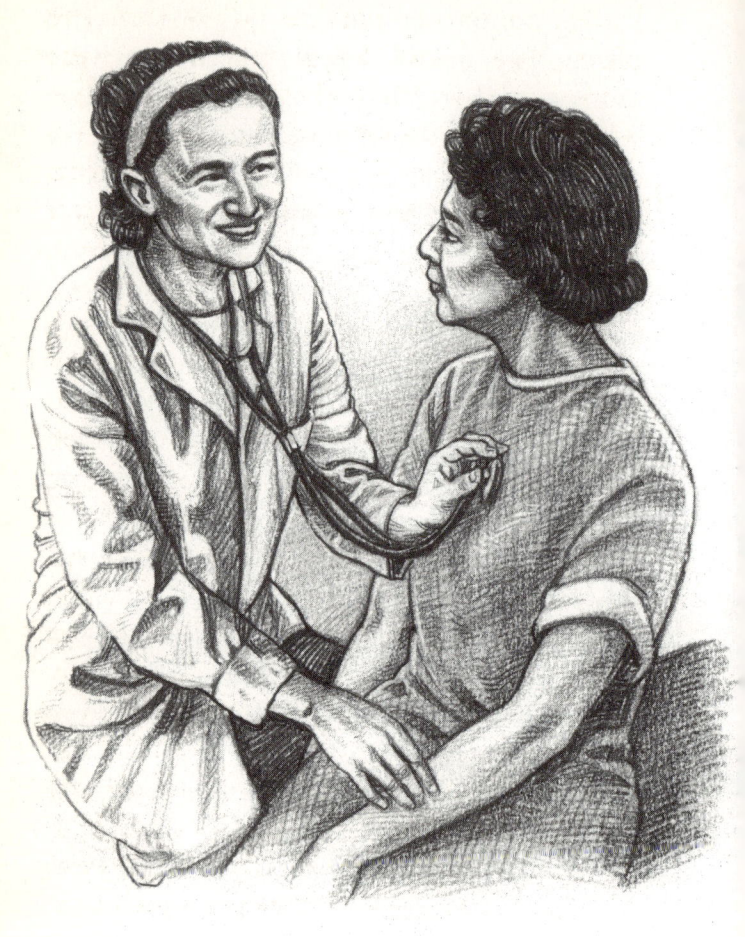

I want to treat each patient as I would treat Jesus.

Daily, numerous patients waited in her office. The doctor knew that many were anxious and worried. She greeted each one with concern and compassion. *I must never appear rushed or tired, she thought. My patients deserve my time and my total attention. I want to treat each person as I would treat Jesus himself.*

Doctor Beretta was well loved by people who were sick and needed medical care. She was like a big sister to the younger women, a mother to the children, and a friend to the older patients. She was genuine and caring with all.

Gianna didn't allow her professional responsibilities, important as they were, to cut into the time she had set aside for prayer. She attended Mass, received Holy Communion, and prayed the Rosary every day. Periods spent in spiritual reading and meditation brought her God's strength and peace.

Pietro's days were just as crowded with activity, but the couple found as much time as they could to enjoy each other's company. In the coolness of many late summer evenings, Gianna and Pietro liked to stroll along scenic routes and enjoy the beauty of nature.

"Don't laugh at me, Pietro, but our engagement has made me feel so happy!" Gianna spontaneously burst out one evening. "Much of each day is ordinary enough, but deep inside me there's an excitement that makes it fuller and more special."

"I know exactly what you mean," Pietro smiled back. "I feel the same way." As they continued their walk, Pietro thought about what Gianna had just said. He suddenly stopped. "Has anyone ever told you that your joy is contagious, Gianna Beretta?"

"No. You're the first, Pietro Molla," Gianna answered with a laugh.

Since I've met Gianna, I've been living on a whole different level, Pietro reflected. *She's made me see how beautiful and full of meaning life really is.*

"What are you thinking, Pietro?" Gianna asked.

"Just that you bring so much happiness into my life," Pietro answered, "so much happiness."

10
Mrs. Molla

"Pietro, I have an idea," Gianna announced one day as their wedding date drew closer.

"You have my full attention," Pietro responded, pretending to look very serious.

"Could we offer a 'spiritual triduum'—three special days of prayer—to prepare for our marriage?"

"I've never heard of anyone doing that, but it sounds like a wonderful plan," Pietro agreed. "What, exactly, did you have in mind?"

"I was thinking that we could attend morning Mass for the three days prior to our wedding to ask God's blessings on our new life together. I realize that we won't be able to go to Mass together because of our work schedules, but that doesn't matter. We'll be together in spirit. I'll go to my usual Mass at the Sanctuary of the Assumption in Magenta . . ."

"And I'll attend the early Mass at Our Lady of Good Counsel in Ponte Nuovo," Pietro broke in enthusiastically.

The couple prayed for each other, for the children they hoped God would send them, and in thanksgiving for the gift of their lives and their Catholic faith. Both were so grateful that God had brought them together.

Saturday, September 24, 1955, dawned clear and sunny. It was a perfect day for a wedding. The pews of Magenta's glorious Basilica of Saint Martin began to fill with eager worshippers. Pink and white carnations adorned the church. The forty-two-year-old groom and his best man and ushers stood expectantly up front where the main aisle ended at the foot of the sanctuary.

Suddenly the reverberating notes of the organ broke the silence. All eyes turned to the entrance of the basilica. The slender bride, a few weeks shy of her thirty-third birthday, stood regally in her white, floor-length satin gown. Gianna's veil accentuated her dark hair and sparkling eyes. With one hand, she carried a beautiful bouquet. Her free arm was looped through that of her brother Ferdinando. Gianna smiled radiantly. The crowd spontaneously began to applaud.

Gianna looked up at her brother: "Thank you, Nando," she whispered.

"You're very welcome, my little sister," he returned with a broad smile.

Gianna walked slowly in step with Nando. The main aisle seemed so long that she wondered if they would ever reach the altar. As they drew nearer to the front of the basilica, Gianna became more aware of the crowd that filled the church. *How good of them all to come,* she thought. *If only Mama and Papa could be here to share our joy.* The tears glistening in her eyes were quickly banished by her next thought. *But you are here, Mama and Papa. I'm carrying you in my heart.*

To add to the joy of the occasion, Father Giuseppe, Gianna's brother, celebrated their wedding Mass. Kneeling together before the altar, Gianna and Pietro vowed to love and remain united to each other forever. It was truly an unforgettable day.

After their honeymoon, the Mollas moved into a lovely home owned by the company for which Pietro worked. The company had made it available to him and his family for as long as he was the manager of La Saffa. Things couldn't have worked out better. The couple would begin their married life in Ponte Nuovo, a short distance from Our Lady of Good Counsel Church.

Because he had so many responsibilities, Pietro had to leave very early for work, but Gianna was overjoyed that she could continue her practice of attending morning Mass. This helped her focus her whole day on loving and serving God. Gianna often reviewed the day to come with the Lord as she waited for Mass to begin. *Prayers, housework, Lord, what else? Oh, today there's also grocery shopping to do, and of course preparing supper. That will take up most of my time.* Then it was off to the office and the day's appointments.

Each person was welcomed warmly. If the patient came regularly, Dr. Molla remembered many particular details about his or her family and medical history. Gianna moved calmly from one person to the next, giving each one her full attention. Soon enough it was time to go home and make dinner. That was a blessing, too, as Gianna was a good cook and enjoyed preparing meals. The young doctor would glance at her watch. *Pietro will be home soon*, she'd think. *I want to have everything just right for him.* With a quick wave to her office staff, Dr. Molla was gone for the day.

11
A Wonderful Surprise

Gianna and Pietro joyfully adjusted to their new lives together, and found meaning and happiness in ordinary life. "Do you know what I most look forward to each day?" Pietro asked Gianna as he set down his briefcase one evening and gave her a kiss.

"What?" she eagerly replied.

"Finding you waiting for me when I come home."

I thought he was going to say that he most appreciated my cooking! Gianna smiled to herself. "Well, dinner is ready, Pietro," she said gently leading him by the hand to the dining room table. "Come and eat before it gets cold."

A candle glowed at the center of the table. Even though Gianna's days were also busy and tiring, she tried to make their dinners at home peaceful and relaxed. She knew it was what her husband needed after a long and pressured day at work. Bowing their heads in prayer, the newlyweds thanked the Lord for his blessings and for the meal they were about to share.

Although there were just the two of them at the table, the couple always found plenty to talk and laugh about. Some evenings, after dinner, Gianna and Pietro would linger to discuss more serious matters. The new husband felt free to share work-related problems with his wife. He valued Gianna's opinions and insights. Gianna, in turn, confided to Pietro the daily joys and challenges she faced as a doctor.

The waning months of 1955 gave way to the New Year 1956. One night, it was Gianna who brought up a more serious topic. "Pietro," she ventured, "today I was offered a position as health director at the Ponte Nuovo children's day-care center and clinic for mothers."

"What do *you* think about that?" her husband asked, watching her face intently.

Gianna's eyes were dancing with anticipation. "Well, I'd really like to accept," she admitted, "if you think it's a good idea."

"I think it's a great idea!" Pietro replied.

"I was hoping you'd say that," Gianna countered. "I'll let them know tomorrow!"

Toward the end of that February, Gianna and Pietro came home from Sunday Mass as usual. Gianna prepared a delicious breakfast. It felt good to be able to sit down and just be with each other without having to worry about rushing off to work.

It is quiet, isn't it? Gianna thought. *Maybe this is the right time . . .* "Pietro, I have a wonderful surprise," she began. "I think you'll be just as thrilled about it as I am."

Pietro eyed her over the rim of his coffee cup. "What is it?" he asked curiously.

"We're going to have a baby!" Gianna joyfully announced.

It took just a split second for Pietro's stunned expression to transform into a broad smile. "That's wonderful, Gianna! Just wonderful! But . . . when?"

"In November, can you believe it? Oh Pietro, let's pray that the pregnancy goes well, and that we'll celebrate the first addition to our little family *this very year*."

The rest of that Sunday seemed like a dream.

The months, busy as they were, flew by. Pietro left the house early each morning. Being the manager of his company brought an impressive daily workload. Not to mention the business trips—some long, some short—which he frequently had to make.

As the days of her pregnancy advanced, Gianna felt more morning nausea. She knew that this was often a normal part of expecting a child, but the pain she was also experiencing was not. Gianna prayed, and placed her concerns in God's hands. She would happily pat her growing stomach and say, "You're worth everything I have to go through. Your father and I can't wait for you to be born!"

Regardless of any discomfort she felt, every morning Gianna would head off to Mass. Returning home, she would have a light breakfast and then leave for work. Rarely did anyone at her medical office notice that the doctor herself was not feeling well. She didn't mention it to Pietro. After all, his job gave him enough to worry about.

She smiled as she opened the door to the day-care center one day. *How many children can benefit from a good pediatrician!* she reflected. Each little patient the gentle Doctor Molla led into her office was made to feel wanted and important. Gianna had a special way with children. She could quickly put them at ease and distract them from their fears.

At other hours, nervous, and sometimes frightened expectant mothers came to her for medical help and advice. "Why don't we pray together for a few moments," the doctor would often invite. "Dear Jesus, I bring this young woman and her baby to you. Please fill them both with your love and courage. Strengthen this mother's desire to bring a new life into the world. Help her to believe in the beauty and sacredness of all human life. Amen."

One particular afternoon, a troubled young woman came to see Dr. Molla. Tears streamed down her cheeks. "I love my baby, Doctor," she confided, "but I'm afraid and confused. I'm not married, and I have no idea how I'm going to support and take care of this baby. I don't know what to do. I've even thought of trying to get an abortion, but I know it's illegal—and also a terrible sin. Can you help me?"

Doctor Molla gave the young mother a gentle hug. "You don't have to be afraid anymore. I'll make sure that you and your baby receive all the help and support you need. Let's put everything into God's hands. Your situation is difficult, but with Jesus, everything will work out." Gianna reached for a tissue and handed it to the expectant mother. "No more tears now," she said softly. "Your baby is a precious gift from God. Together you and I will prepare to receive him or her. Think about that little life within you and be happy! All right?"

"All right," the young woman smiled in relief.

12

THE FIRST "TREASURES" ARRIVE!

Monday, November 19, 1956, was a thrilling day for Gianna and Pietro. It was the day they welcomed their first child into the world. At that time, no one knew whether an expectant mother was going to have a boy or a girl until the baby was born. Every birth was a surprise. Born at home with the help of Gianna's brother, Dr. Ferdinando, the baby was a little boy. Gianna and Pietro had had animated discussions about what to call their child if he were a boy. The name came easily: Pierluigi.

Pierluigi slept peacefully on his parents' bed, snuggled in his mother's protective arms. Relatives on both sides of the family came and went bringing their good wishes, gifts, and promises of prayers. "Isn't he beautiful!" they declared in hushed tones. "Just like a little angel. He'll bring you much joy!"

Pietro was beside himself with excitement and pride.

"Wouldn't you like to hold your son?" Gianna smilingly asked.

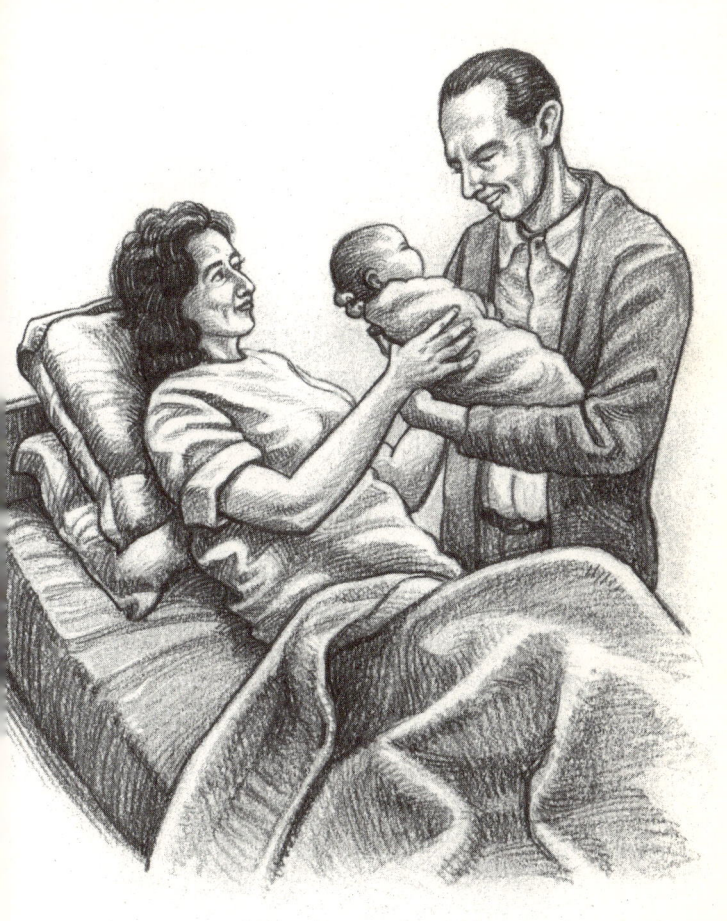

"Wouldn't you like to hold your son?"

"Yes,". Pietro eagerly replied, "but I don't want to hurt him. He looks so small . . ."

Gianna chuckled. "He'll be just fine," she assured, as she held the baby out to Pietro. "Go ahead, take him."

Pietro sat down carefully with his precious bundle. He studied the dark eyes, now opened. He stroked the curly, sandy head of hair, the little turned up nose and rosy lips. He gazed in wonder at the baby's tiny, perfectly formed ears. "What a joy it will be for us to watch our son grow!" Pietro exclaimed.

The happy mother nodded. Her eyes were growing heavy. *Pierluigi is right at home with his Papa*, she thought. *And Mama is going to take a nap.*

Just as each child who would follow, Pierluigi's Baptism was held at the Church of Our Lady of Good Counsel just a few days after he was born. His uncle, Father Giuseppe, celebrated the rite. For Gianna, it was important that every one of their children be consecrated to the Blessed Mother. Starting with Pierluigi, Pietro began a tradition of praying aloud the act of consecration to Our Lady of Good Counsel after the baptismal ceremony. The Mollas cherished this devotion to their heavenly mother and wanted to place each of their children under her special protection. After the Baptism, Gianna and Pietro prayed for their new baby. "O Holy Virgin Mary, Our Lady of Good Counsel . . . you are the mother of divine grace and the advocate of sinners . . . Be our son's counselor and guide . . . Through the Precious Blood of your Son, help him receive the forgiveness of his sins, and everything he will need for the salvation of his soul. . . ."

Gianna and Pietro missed Pierluigi during the days they worked. But they knew he was in safe hands with his aunt Zita and Savina Passeri, a young woman whom they hired as a housekeeper. In spite of their busy work schedules, the couple was committed to spending time with each other and with Pierluigi. The infant had a cheerful disposition and enough energy to overwhelm a whole room full of grownups. He also knew how to entertain. As he began to toddle, reaching from one piece of furniture to the next, Pierluigi would smile and look around to see if anyone was appreciating his hard work. When Gianna was at home, the little boy always had his eyes on her. Once he could get around, he followed her everywhere. He found this very amusing. Mama did, too.

By Pierluigi's first birthday, Gianna and Pietro had some exciting news for him. "Jesus has a special gift for Pierluigi," Gianna told him. "Soon he is going to send you a new baby to love and play with!"

Pierluigi's eyes grew wide with delight. "Baby!" he repeated with glee, waving his pudgy arms. "Baby for me!"

On Wednesday, December 11, 1957, Pierluigi's new little sister arrived. She was born at home just as her older brother had been. Pietro and Pierluigi had been kept outside the room until the new baby was born. Thirteen-month-old Pierluigi was anxious to see her—and his mother. Pietro had his hands full trying to keep him calm and quiet until Dr. Ferdinando let them into the bedroom.

Pierluigi rushed ahead of his father to the bedside. He reached out his small hand and patted his Mama's arm. Babbling happily all the while, Pierluigi watched approvingly as the tiny baby slept. Although she was so little, she already had an impressive head of hair.

"This is your new little sister," Gianna joyfully announced. "Do you want to know her name?" The little boy nodded his head in excitement. "She's Maria Zita, but we're going to call her Mariolina," Gianna said. "Do you like that name?" Pierluigi nodded his head "yes" again. He was thrilled with everything.

That Christmas of 1957 was an especially happy one for Gianna and Pietro. What pleasure it gave them to watch Pierluigi being so attentive to his new little sister. Mariolina, for her part, had been their perfect Christmas gift. *My children are truly my treasures,* Gianna thought. *How can I ever thank you, Lord, for entrusting them to me!*

13

LIFE IS BEAUTIFUL

The Molla home was always open and friendly. There was discipline and order, but also much joy. Balance was an important part of Gianna and Pietro's life and their children could readily sense that. The couple wanted to raise their family according to the example their own parents had left them. "My parents believed in education by persuasion," Gianna confided to Pietro. "They always spoke respectfully to us, and did their best to help us understand things without becoming impatient or angry. Pietro, that's the kind of mother I want to be."

"I totally agree," her husband said firmly. "My parents were like that, too. They lived in a way that showed us that life is a gift of God to be respected and appreciated."

As busy as they were with their own family and careers, Gianna and Pietro made the effort to keep up with their friends and relatives. Gianna often wrote letters to her siblings who lived far away and visited those nearer to home. Dr. "Nando," her brother, lived close by. His daughter, Iuccia, enjoyed her cousins Pierluigi and Mariolina, and the three had hours of fun together.

Toward the end of 1958, Gianna and Pietro had good news once again—they were expecting another child. The couple was excited. This time, however, Gianna had even more serious problems than she had had during her first two pregnancies. What made it even more difficult was the fact that Pietro had to take an important—and very long—business trip to America. While Gianna understood why he had to be away for nearly eight weeks, she missed Pietro so much that she wrote thirty-one letters to him.

A month before the baby was due to be born, while Pietro was still away, Gianna found herself in danger of losing their baby. Hot with fever and experiencing sharp pains, Gianna telephoned her brother Dr. Ferdinando.

"Get to St. Gerard's Hospital right away!" he urged. "I'll have Dr. Vitali waiting there for you."

The hands of the large wall clock read midnight as Gianna was whisked into the emergency room. *Please, Lord,* she prayed, *save my baby! Please don't let anything happen to my baby!*

The doctor went into action immediately. There was no time to lose. Gianna was given oxygen, tranquilizers, and fluid injections. The treatment was successful. Gianna's fever disappeared and the pains stopped. Two days later, Gianna, feeling almost back to normal, drove to the airport in Milan to bring Pietro home from his long business trip. Only then did Gianna tell him about the frightening experience she had been through.

On July 15, 1959, less than a month after Pietro's return, Laura was born at home. Gianna was thirty-seven at the time. Lauretta was late in coming, just as her brother and sister had been. "What a good baby," Gianna wrote to one of her friends with pride. "She sleeps, eats a little, and almost never cries. She has a full head of black hair and light-colored eyes. She weighs eight pounds and eleven ounces."

Pierluigi and Mariolina were staying with relatives at the Molla's vacation home in Courmayeur, a beautiful little Italian village on the sunny slope of Mont Blanc near the border of Switzerland. This gave Gianna and the new baby time to rest. But Gianna missed her older two children and they missed her. Because there was a phone in their cottage, the children called home each evening. Pierluigi had the most to say. "I want to talk to my new baby sister," he announced one night. "Please put her on the phone." His parents stifled laughs and tried to explain that baby Laura was too little to hold a conversation. Pierluigi accepted that answer, but he wasn't really convinced.

Gianna, Pietro, and Laura soon joined Pierluigi and Mariolina in Courmayeur. The two- and three-year-olds were very excited to meet their baby sister, and Pietro was able to remain in the mountain village with his family for the entire Italian vacation month of August. The family enjoyed these precious days together and spent as much time as they could outdoors. After Pietro had to go back to work, Gianna and the children stayed in Courmayeur until the end of that September. By the time they returned home to Ponte Nuovo, the children's appetites had grown and their faces had become golden and ruddy from the sun and fresh Alpine air.

14

A Time for Joy

Occasionally, Gianna accompanied Pietro on his business trips. In December of 1960, the couple traveled to England and Holland. They enjoyed the opportunity to take in the sights and spend time together. "Thank God for your sister Zita," Pietro declared as they left their hotel one morning.

"Yes," Gianna smiled back. "We don't have to worry about the children knowing that they're in her hands. Her willingness to help makes it possible for us to spend this time together."

For their part, the three "treasures" eagerly gathered around Aunt Zita's telephone each evening waiting for it to ring. They knew who the callers would be: Mama and Papa! Aunt Zita would first give a short report about each of the children, assuring their parents that all was well. Then it was Pierluigi's turn. As the oldest, he insisted that he get to speak with each of his parents. He also wanted a kiss from them over the telephone. Only then was he happy.

Gianna loved being a mother. She enjoyed attending to the needs of her children and continually showed them her affection. "Pierluigi, you're the big brother," she'd say, patting him gently on the head. "Mariolina, come to Mama, your dress needs to be straightened. *Now* you look like a princess! Shhhh, it's all right, Lauretta. Soon you'll be asleep," Gianna smiled as she whispered.

Gianna once wrote to her husband who was in New York. "Pierluigi never fails to recite a Hail Mary for you. He ends it with, 'Please come back soon, Papa!' Mariolina helps by folding her little hands in prayer and sending up kisses to Mother Mary."

On another occasion, Pierluigi was in the back yard with Gianna. As he watched her hanging clothes on the line, he asked, "Where is Papa?"

"He's in another country doing some important work for his company," Gianna explained.

"But how did he get there?" Pierluigi questioned.

"He flew on a big airplane," Gianna replied.

The little boy quietly thought about that amazing answer. Not long after, a large plane flew over the house. "Mama!" Pierluigi yelled, jumping up and down. "There goes Papa! Wave to him! Wave to Papa!"

Gianna took Pierluigi and Mariolina to Mass when Pietro was away. On one particular Sunday, Gianna's brother, Father Giuseppe, was the celebrant. The priest's other nieces and nephews had joined the congregation as well. Father Giuseppe gave all of them a special blessing. Gianna later wrote to Pietro, "Mariolina was peaceful and very well behaved, but not Pierluigi. He really couldn't take more than five minutes worth of church."

Gianna's joy was centered in her marriage and family life. Both she and Pietro had come from larger families, and had happy memories of a home filled with brothers and sisters. This was reflected in their own desire to welcome all the children God would send them. "Gianna's wish to have a big family like the one we grew up in was always alive in her," her sister, Sister Virginia, once explained.

Gianna loved life and all that was beautiful—nature, music, sports, art, and even fashion! She gave God credit for everything that was wonderful about the world. She wanted to share life, joy, and beauty with her children. She often repeated, "Children are blessings." Pietro wholeheartedly agreed.

Gianna's dedication as a wife, mother, and doctor required a strong commitment. She found the strength she needed rooted in her deep faith—faith that had become as much a part of her as her very breath. Gianna's daily decisions flowed from her Catholic beliefs, and from her love for God.

But a time was coming that would test Gianna's faith. Dark clouds would attempt to overshadow her joy.

15

THE WAY OF THE CROSS

"Pietro, God has blessed us again!" Gianna exclaimed with excitement. "I'm expecting another child!"

"Our fourth treasure," Pietro responded with delight as he gave her a hug.

At first, all went well during that summer of 1961. But, after several weeks, Gianna developed some unusual swelling. She was also experiencing a great deal of pain. She knew that something was wrong. She immediately made an appointment to be examined by her brother, Dr. Ferdinando. The news wasn't good.

"Gianna, you have a large tumor growing very close to the area where the baby is," Ferdinando told her. "I'm sending you to Dr. Vitali for a second opinion, but I think the tumor will have to be removed—and soon."

Dr. Vitali agreed that the tumor needed to come out. "There are three different ways of eliminating the tumor," he explained to Gianna and Pietro. "The first method would be the safest for Gianna. It would involve removing not only the tumor but the entire area around it as well. However, you would never be able to have children again, and ..." the doctor's voice grew low, "your two-month-old unborn baby would die as an undesired side effect of the surgery."

Gianna tightened her grip on Pietro's hand. They knew that in this very rare case such an operation would not be a sin because even though their baby would die, the purpose of the surgery was *not* to kill the child, but to save the mother's life.

"What is our second option, Doctor?" Pietro quietly asked.

"The second type of surgery would allow you to have other children," Dr. Vitali continued. "We would have to remove the tumor—and abort the baby."

"Oh, no, Doctor! We could never do that! We would *never* abort our child! We are Catholics!" Gianna exclaimed. She knew that any procedure that would intentionally end the life of their unborn baby was against God's law. "What is our final option?"

"The third type of surgery would remove only the tumor. It might save your baby and allow you to have more children later on. But there are no guarantees," the doctor stressed, "and it would put your own life in danger, Gianna, now and in the future. You could have serious and dangerous complications from such an operation, and you might lose this baby anyway."

Being a doctor herself, Gianna clearly understood the decision she would have to make. A few days later, she made the most generous choice, and opted for the third method of surgery out of love for the life of her unborn baby. To Dr. Vitali, Ferdinando, and Pietro, Gianna pleaded, "Save our baby! Whatever happens during the operation, please respect my wishes and do everything you can to save our baby!"

Gianna underwent surgery on September 6, 1961. The tumor was successfully removed, and Gianna recuperated little by little. She soon went back to her work as a mother and doctor. But there were still seven months before the couple's baby would be ready to be born, and no guarantees about whether Gianna and the baby would both remain safe.

Who knows how many times during those months Gianna thought of Dr. Vitali's warning and the medical complications that could cause a miscarriage or her own death. It was as if Gianna were walking her own long way of the cross. Yet with unshakeable hope Gianna trusted God with everything, and went about the responsibilities of her life in peace.

Jesus, she prayed and asked others to pray, *please let our baby be born safe and healthy. Please . . . I'm putting everything in your hands.*

"Gianna! What on earth have you been doing?" Pietro asked in amazement when he arrived home one evening. A clothes closet was completely empty. Shirts, dresses, and pairs of slacks were spread all over the bed and nearby chairs.

"I've just been tidying up," Gianna answered with a tired smile.

"Tidying up?" Pietro repeated in disbelief. "This looks more like major spring cleaning. You shouldn't be doing all this now . . . especially during *this* pregnancy."

"It's nothing, Pietro," Gianna replied, trying to sound very casual. "I only want everything to be nice and orderly before I leave for the hospital."

Gianna had decided to prepare herself for whatever would happen. While she hoped and prayed for the best, she had accepted the possibility that she might die in childbirth. Every day Gianna continued her "cleaning." She went through every drawer, each closet, each and every knick-knack and photo. She made sure every article of her family's clothing was neatly folded and in its proper place. Every day Pietro noticed that some other area of the house had been set in perfect order. Perhaps Gianna sensed something that Pietro did not? Pietro grew worried . . . too worried to ask her about it.

16

Good Friday

The fact that Gianna had had surgery early in the pregnancy meant that it was too risky for her to give birth at home. When it was time for the baby to be born, Pietro drove her to St. Gerard's Hospital. It was the afternoon of April 20, 1962—Good Friday.

On the way there, Gianna suddenly turned to her husband with concern and an urgent request. "Pietro, promise me that if the doctors can save only one of us, you will choose the baby. Remember, if you have to decide between the baby and me, save our baby!"

Pietro fought back his tears and struggled to control his voice. "Yes, Gianna, I promise," he hoarsely replied.

Gianna's dark eyes could not hide her suffering, but she was determined to remain at peace. Remembering how joyful the births of their other children had been, she realized that this baby's birth was going to be difficult and painful. She also knew that there was a chance she would need to undergo surgery again. Still, Gianna trusted

"Remember, Pietro, if you have to decide between the baby and me, save our baby!"

God. She knew that he would take care of her and her family. He always had. Ready to accept whatever would happen, Gianna quietly told one of the nurses without letting Pietro hear, "Sister, this time I have come here to die."

For the rest of the day and all through the night, Gianna prayed that the baby would be born. But as dawn approached, it became clear that surgery was going to be necessary to deliver the baby. The doctors had Gianna prepared for the operation on Holy Saturday morning. The nurses attending her were surprised to see Gianna so calm. In fact, they even asked her if she was the patient waiting for surgery or if it was one of the other nearby women! Pietro stood by Gianna's side as long as he was allowed. He bent to kiss her before the nurses wheeled her into the operating room. "I love you so much, Gianna," he whispered. "I'll be praying for you and our baby with all my heart."

Gianna smiled bravely. "And you know how much I love you, my Pietro," she whispered back.

At 11:00 am that Holy Saturday morning, a healthy, beautiful baby girl was born. She weighed almost ten pounds. The infant, whom Gianna and Pietro named Gianna Emanuela, was cradled by the exhausted mother. Gianna pressed the baby to herself. She gazed at her with indescribable love for a long time without uttering a word.

A few hours passed. Then the agony began. Gianna's temperature soared, and she started to experience excruciating pains. The doctors rushed to find a diagnosis. "She has developed septic peritonitis," Dr. Vitali sadly informed Pietro. "It's an extremely serious and fast-moving infection. She may have contracted it somehow during surgery. We're using very strong antibiotics to try and overcome it. I don't know if we'll be successful . . ." As the nurses took the newborn back to the nursery, Gianna spoke to her in her heart. *I'm afraid that I may not live to see you grow up, my little one, but how I love you!*

Hour by hour, the infection and pain worsened. Pietro never left Gianna's bedside. Holding her hand, he gently stroked her burning forehead. Because of her own medical training, Gianna understood exactly what was happening to her. Even though her suffering was severe, she chose not to take any medications that would put her to sleep. She wanted to remain conscious, and as present to the people she loved as she could be. In her extreme pain, Gianna began to call out for help to her mother, who had died twenty years earlier. She repeated the names of her children. She prayed over and over again, "Jesus, I love you. Jesus, help me!"

Gianna spent all of Easter Sunday, Monday, and Tuesday in anguish. As the infection worsened, she grew weaker. On Tuesday, Sister Virginia—her sister and best friend—arrived home from her medical mission in India. "Finally, you're here, Virginia!" Gianna exclaimed as the nun entered the hospital room. "If only you knew what it means to face death knowing that you are leaving four little children behind!" Virginia's eyes filled with tears as she bent to caress Gianna.

Gianna tried to console her husband. "I know that I'm dying," she whispered with tears welling up in her eyes. "Poor Pietro! You'll have to raise our four treasures without me. But don't worry. I've already asked my sister Zita to help you. Promise me you won't worry, my Pietro. I don't want you to be troubled."

Children, especially young children, were not permitted to visit family members in the hospital. While they were being taken care of by relatives, Gianna missed them terribly.

On Wednesday night, Gianna made a special request. "Pietro, I'd like to die at home. Please . . . take me home. Perhaps I'll be able to see our treasures one last time."

Pietro brushed away the tears he could no longer hold back. "I'll bring you home, Gianna," he promised, "just as soon as the doctors give their permission."

Not long after, Gianna's condition became so grave that Dr. Vitali forbade her to have any visitors other than Sister Virginia, who was also a doctor. Even Pietro, numb with pain and sorrow, now had to wait outside the hospital room door with Gianna's brothers and sister and the chaplain. This new sacrifice was especially difficult for Gianna. "Virginia, where are Pietro, and Zita, and Nando? And Father Giuseppe, and Francisco?" she asked Sister Virginia in a worried tone. "Why don't they come to see me anymore?"

"They're right outside the door," Sister Virginia soothed. "Dr. Vitali says you need your rest. He'll let them in once you're feeling a little stronger."

Gianna's family members weren't the only ones waiting in the hallway. Her friends and patients had also lined up, hoping for a last chance to see her. But Gianna never improved enough to have visitors. She accepted this added pain of their absence with faith.

In those final days, Gianna's brother, Father Giuseppe, administered the Anointing of the Sick to his dying sister. Gianna, who had always tried to attend daily Mass, and who loved receiving Jesus in the Holy Eucharist, could now no longer swallow. "At least touch the sacred Host to my lips," she pleaded.

Gianna raised her eyes to the crucifix hanging on the wall. She offered her suffering to the Lord who had suffered so much for us. *Now I understand a little of what it must have been like for you, Jesus,* she prayed. *You too died so alone—except for Mary and St. John—on Calvary. Jesus I love you! Help me to accept death, Jesus! Help me to die in a holy way!*

17
Going Home

"Gianna has fallen into a coma. It is not likely that she will awaken from it," Dr. Vitali quietly explained to Pietro on Friday, April 27. "If you wish, you may bring her home."

"Yes, Doctor," the grief-stricken husband replied. "I must bring her home. That's what she wanted."

An ambulance sat outside the hospital before dawn on Saturday morning, its motor running in readiness. Pietro and Sister Virginia watched as Gianna was gently lifted into the vehicle.

Gianna, motionless and weak, was soon back in her own house and bed. In a nearby room, her three older children were just waking up. Gianna Emanuela—only eight days old—was still in the hospital. The children, seeing their father and aunts and uncles and the commotion around their parents' bedroom, realized that their mother was home. "Mama! Mama!" they excitedly cried out, hoping to see her.

It's possible, as Pietro later said, that Gianna could hear the children, although she couldn't make any response. Pietro decided that it was best to send the little ones to a relative's house. Soon the house grew silent. The "treasures" were elsewhere.

Pietro stayed by Gianna's side. Though he wasn't sure how he would find the strength to go on, he realized that Gianna's life would end soon. Pietro recalled the day they had met, and the joy she had brought to his life. He remembered the excitement of their engagement, and how beautiful a bride Gianna had been on their wedding day. Although Gianna could not speak, Pietro could hear her comforting voice. *Be grateful, Pietro. God has been so good to us! Look at the treasures he has given us!* His heart was full. At 8:00 AM that Saturday morning, Gianna died. The loving and dedicated wife, mother, and medical doctor was just thirty-nine years old.

While Pietro and the children were still mourning Gianna, the news of her death was traveling through the neighborhoods.

People began to arrive at the Molla's front door. Gianna was placed in a room where she could be seen by everyone who came to pay their respects. As was the custom, each visitor brought a candle and placed it near her casket. Quietly, respectfully, they filed by the woman who, even in death, looked serene and beautiful. "She was so young to die," the mourners murmured to each other. "So young and so good."

Some whispered short prayers. Others touched Gianna's face gently with their rosary beads or handkerchiefs. Everyone sensed that she was special. An unbroken line of visitors continued throughout Saturday night, all day and night Sunday, and Monday up until the time of the funeral.

On Sunday afternoon, while the mourners continued to pay tribute to Gianna in her home, Pietro and the rest of the family slipped quietly away. They walked to their small parish church of Our Lady of Good Counsel carrying Gianna Emanuela, who was all dressed in white. Gianna had planned the Baptism of Gianna Emanuela before she died. "I know my wife would want us to go ahead with the Baptism," Pietro explained to their relatives.

The family gathered around the baptismal font. The lovely baby girl rested in the arms of Aunt Zita, Gianna's sister. Father Giuseppe, Gianna's brother, using water from a basin held by Pierluigi, poured water over the infant's head while pronouncing the sacramental formula, "I baptize you Giovanna Emanuela in the name of the Father, and of the Son, and of the Holy Spirit. Amen." As he had done with their other three children, Pietro then consecrated the baby to Our Lady of Good Counsel. The grieving husband and father could sense that the baby's mother was present, too, unseen, but *really* there. *I feel your love, Gianna, even in this great sorrow of mine*, Pietro whispered in his heart.

The family and friends walked the short distance back to the Molla home. Pierluigi stayed close to his father. Back at the house, the little boy kept his eyes on his mother in the coffin.

"Papa," Pierluigi asked, "Why is Mama in that box? Is it *really* Mama? Can she see me and touch me? Can she think about me?"

Pietro gazed lovingly at the little face twisted with confusion. He wanted to answer, but the words just wouldn't come.

Pierluigi rubbed a chubby hand against his cheek to wipe away a tear. "Papa," he added after a moment, "I know what we should do! We should make a little golden house for Mama."

Pietro bent down and picked up his grieving five-and-a-half-year-old son. He hugged him tightly. Pierluigi hugged him back.

18

LOVED FOREVER

Gianna's funeral was scheduled for the afternoon of Monday, April 30. Her coffin was covered with red roses, a symbol of Pietro's love for her.

The mourners—friends, relatives, and admirers—quickly filled the pews of Our Lady of Good Counsel Church. Still the crowds grew. It became obvious that the little church wouldn't be able to hold the great number of people who came. Many fervently followed the Mass from outside.

After the Mass, it was time to bring Gianna to the cemetery. A group of priests walked first. Next came the pallbearers, who carried Gianna's coffin on their shoulders as a sign of respect. Beside the coffin on either side were women with lighted candles. Directly behind the coffin walked Pietro holding Pierluigi and Mariolina by the hand. Laura was still too small to keep up. The Beretta family members and the rest of the people followed.

As the procession made its way to the cemetery, Gianna was carried past her home for the last time. *What a wonderful, happy life we had together*, Pietro thought. *I will love you forever, Gianna*.

It was the custom to place the coffins of deceased persons in small cemetery chapels specially built to honor and remember them. Since Pietro didn't have one, Gianna was given a place in the tomb reserved for priests until the Molla family chapel could be built. Her body remained there for three years. In November of 1965 she was moved to the new chapel that Pietro had built after Mariolina died unexpectedly at the age of six. Remembering Pierluigi's request that they "make Mama a little golden house," Pietro had one wall of the chapel covered with a beautiful mosaic with a brilliant background of gold. The mosaic shows Gianna, Mariolina, and Pietro's sister Teresina standing before Our Lady of Lourdes.

Sister Virginia wrote later to Father Alberto, her missionary brother in Brazil. "Gianna's funeral was very beautiful. In fact, it was impressive, something out of the ordinary. What respect people have for our Gianna! It seems that many people felt a strong desire to go to Confession before paying their final respects to her. 'So many

Confessions!' the amazed parish priest told me. 'So much renewed hope in the mercy of God!' The mourners spoke of Gianna, too," Sister Virginia continued, "about how courageous and self-sacrificing she was. Many said that they want to become as close to God as she was."

Doctor Ferdinando shook his head as he gazed out his office window and thought about his sister. *I can't believe that I won't be hearing her soft, kind voice, or seeing her beautiful smile again in this life. She always believed I'd make a good doctor . . .*

A baby's wails from the waiting room broke into his thoughts. "Now there's a sign of life and vigor," he chuckled, "a reminder that I have a room full of patients waiting for me." Rising from his desk he thought again. *You know, I can almost hear Gianna saying, "Nando, what are you doing sitting around? Get back to work!"*

The doctor entered the waiting room. He greeted the first patient and ushered her into the examination room. Persons came and went. As the day wore on, Ferdinando felt almost as if his sister was there with him. He seemed to hear Gianna's voice again. It was unmistakable. "Nando, I have so much pain . . ." He traveled back in memory to that midnight when Gianna had been rushed to the hospital, with Pietro away on a business trip. *While the specialist and staff worked feverishly to save you, Gianna, I prayed,* he told her in his heart. *You don't know how much I prayed! I wanted you to live. And you did, a while longer, but not long enough . . . It's strange, Gianna, but I can still feel your presence and your love. Help me to be the kind of doctor you were.*

More than anyone else, Pietro felt surrounded by Gianna's presence. Their four children reminded him of Gianna constantly. They were so much like her, trying hard to be good and finding joy in everything. Gianna's sister Zita, along with Pietro's mother and sister helped him to raise the four little ones.

Aunt Zita soon realized that the children loved to listen to her stories about their mother. Even tiny Gianna Emanuela would follow the sounds and watch Zita's facial expressions. "I remember when your Mama was little," Zita told the children one day. "She would have been your size, Mariolina, and just about your age." The excited listener held up four fingers just to make sure her aunt knew how old she was.

"Today I'll tell you about how much your Mama loved Jesus," Zita went on. "She showed it in many ways. When she was a teenager, she went to visit the pastor of our parish. She asked him, 'How can I love and please Jesus more?' Monsignor was very kind and thoughtful. 'You know, Gianna,' he said, 'we can make short visits to Jesus in the Blessed Sacrament. We can also keep a little diary . . .'"

"What's that?" Pierluigi interrupted.

"It's a notebook or a tablet of paper," Zita explained. "It can be small enough to fit into your pocket or larger, like a book. You can use it to write down things that helped you grow closer to Jesus, or about times when you could have been better. Your Mama wrote things like that in her diary."

Aunt Zita's little audience was speechless. Pierluigi finally broke the silence. "Our Mama was very, very good, wasn't she?" he asked.

Aunt Zita smiled. "Yes, I think she was. But she was too busy seeing the good in everyone else to notice."

19

Pro-Life Saint

As Pietro was coming out of church one day, he came face-to-face with a young couple he had never met. The woman stepped forward. "Sir," she asked, "are you by any chance Doctor Gianna Molla's widower?"

Pietro smiled. "Yes," he replied.

"We'd like you to know something," the wife quietly continued, glancing at her husband.

He nodded. "Yes, Mr. Molla. We've heard about your wife and we wanted to tell you how much her story has meant to us. Her total dedication to your marriage and family and her witness to the sacredness and value of all human life . . . these things really inspire us."

"What we're trying to say is that we hope our marriage will be holy, too," the young woman added enthusiastically.

"Thank you so much," was all Pietro could answer. His eyes filled with tears as he turned to walk away. It felt good to know that their marriage, and the way they had lived it, was encouraging young families to live their faith. *Even now, Gianna,* he thought, *you're still serving others.*

There was profound sadness at losing Gianna. But there was joy, too, because of the good that was already coming from her life and example. On the first anniversary of Gianna's death, Father Olinto Marella, a family friend who had been at her bedside in her last days, had an idea. *Gianna's life is a gift to all of us,* he thought. *Wouldn't it be wonderful if more people knew about this holy woman?* He decided to pay Pietro a visit. "I'd like to write a pamphlet about your wife," Father Marella told him. "I really believe her story can inspire others."

Pietro hesitated. Shy and reserved, he was reluctant to have the joys and sorrows he had shared with Gianna made public. But, in the end, he gave in. "All right, Father," Pietro told him, "write your pamphlet if you must, but please don't give it too wide a circulation."

Little by little, the story of Gianna's life spread. More and more people began to talk about her holiness. In the spring of 1970, eight years after Gianna's death, Bishop Carlo Colombo visited Pietro's parish to celebrate the sacrament of Confirmation.

"Mr. Molla," he told Pietro, "the Church would like to open the cause of your wife's beatification. But we need your approval to begin. Will you give us permission?"

Pietro was speechless. *My Gianna, a saint!* he thought. After some reflection, Pietro had his answer for the bishop. "Yes, Your Excellency, if you feel that Gianna's example will help other mothers and families, go ahead." The official process of beatification began. Gianna's patients, friends, and relatives were interviewed, her many letters were read, and the choices she had made were evaluated. As more people learned about Gianna, some asked her to pray for their needs. When healings occurred, some people gave the credit to Gianna's intercession. These claims were also investigated.

Gianna was beatified by Pope John Paul II in Rome on April 24, 1994, during the International Year of the Family that had been proclaimed by the United Nations and celebrated by the Church. The miracle accepted for her beatification was experienced by a mother in the very hospital which Gianna's brother, Father Alberto, had opened in Brazil. This woman, Mrs. Lucia Cirilo, had a baby who died before birth. Afterward, she developed a dangerous infection. She needed to be transferred to a larger hospital, which could perform a necessary operation. But the specialized hospital was far away, and time was running out. The doctors feared that Mrs. Cirilo wouldn't survive the trip. A Sister nurse began praying to God for a healing through the intercession of Gianna. She asked the other nurses to pray, too. The following day, the patient was completely cured! Mrs. Cirilo attended Gianna's beatification ceremony in Rome, where she met and spoke with Pietro.

A second miracle, required for Gianna's canonization, was also received by a mother. She was from Italy, and her name was Elisabete Comparini. When Elisabete was expecting her third child, something went terribly wrong. After three months, the fluid that must surround an unborn baby suddenly dropped to a low level. Then it totally disappeared. This normally would have resulted in the baby's death. But Elisabete and her husband prayed that Gianna would intercede with God for them. Their perfectly healthy baby girl was born in May of 2000. They named her Gianna Maria.

Pope John Paul II canonized Gianna Beretta Molla on May 16, 2004, in Saint

Peter's Square. Her feast day is April 28, the date on which she died. Present at the canonization ceremony were Pietro, her 91-year-old husband, as well as Pierluigi, Laura, and Gianna Emanuela, her three living children, a brother and sister, and many other relatives, friends, and former patients. It was the first time in the history of the Church that a saint's own spouse had attended the saint's canonization.

Although many widows have been canonized, Gianna is the first married laywoman ever to be declared a saint. She is also the first canonized female physician.

It's important for us to remember that Saint Gianna died a heroic death because she *lived* a heroic life. She chose life and love every day as a wife, mother, and doctor. She spent her life caring unselfishly for the lives of others, and accepted whatever God allowed. She trusted him completely, and placed everything in his hands.

Gianna is a very special pro-life saint for us today. When so many in our world do not respect the value and dignity of the human person, her life story teaches us the truth: *each and every human life is sacred*—from the youngest unborn baby to the oldest person on earth. Each life is a precious gift from God, and each human person is created in God's own image.

If Saint Gianna were here today, she would have a special message for you—"Your life is a gift!"

She might also ask a question . . . "How are *you* going to live it?"

Prayer

Saint Gianna, you've taught us—not only with words, but through your example—some very important truths. One is that God wants all our families to be centers of love. Remind me that the love and understanding I practice in my own family can help to make the world a better place.

You've also shown us that every unborn baby is a precious and unrepeatable gift of God whose life should never be taken away. Saint Gianna, ask God that all people may come to understand and believe this. Remind me to pray every day for an end to abortion. I want to do what I can to respect and protect the life of each and every person because every human being has been created by God in his own image.

Saint Gianna, you loved life. You knew it was a great gift. Help me to know what God wishes me to do with my life; to spend it well and for the good of others, just as you did. You found joy by trusting God in everything. Help me to do the same. Please pray for me. Amen.

Glossary

1. Abortion—the deliberate killing of an unborn child. Abortion is a very serious sin against the Fifth Commandment, "You shall not kill." To **abort** a baby means to perform an abortion.

2. Anointing of the Sick—the sacrament by which Jesus gives spiritual comfort, strength, peace, and sometimes physical help to someone who is seriously ill due to sickness, injury, or advanced age. God's Spirit, through this sacrament, forgives sin and heals the soul.

3. Basilica—a large church of special importance that is patterned after a type of ancient Roman building.

4. Beatification—the ceremony in which the Catholic Church recognizes that a deceased person lived a life of Gospel holiness in a heroic way. This is done after the person's life and holiness have been fully researched. When we pray to someone who is a candidate for beatification, he or she prays to God for us. In most cases, a proven miracle obtained through the holy person's prayers to God is required for beatification. A person who has been beatified is given the title "Blessed."

5. Blessed Sacrament—another name for the Holy Eucharist, the real Body and Blood of the risen Jesus present under the appearances of bread and wine at Mass. The name Blessed Sacrament is especially used to refer to the Holy Eucharist kept, in the form of consecrated Hosts, in the tabernacle.

6. Canonization—the ceremony in which the Pope solemnly declares that someone is a saint in heaven. To canonize a person is to recognize that he or she has lived a life of heroic virtue, is worthy of imitation, and can intercede with God for us. Like beatification, which must come first, canonization requires a miracle resulting from the holy person's prayers to God.

7. Catechism—a book that explains the truths of our Catholic faith so that we may live by them and grow closer to God.

8. Chaplain—someone, often a priest, who ministers to a certain group of people, for example, to patients in a hospital.

9. Consecrate—to set aside a person or an object for God or God's service. It can also mean, as in this story, to dedicate oneself in a special way to the Blessed Mother.

10. Diocesan priest—any priest who is not a member of a religious order but lives and works in a specific diocese in obedience to his bishop.

11. Miracle—a wonderful happening that goes beyond the powers of nature and is produced by God to teach us some truth or to testify to the holiness of a person.

12. Miscarriage—the death of an unborn baby in the womb due to natural causes.

13. Mission—(as used in this story) a central location from which a priest and his helpers would not only bring the message of Jesus to the people of a certain area for the first time, but also minister to their needs. While always including a chapel or church for the celebration of Mass, a mission could also include a school or clinic for the sick.

14. Missionary—a priest, sister, brother, or layperson who brings Jesus' Gospel message to others. Many missionaries travel to foreign countries to teach people about Jesus and the Catholic Church he founded.

15. Mont Blanc—"White Mountain" in French. Mont Blanc is the highest mountain in the Alps. It gets its name from the fact that it is always covered with snow.

16. Mosaic—a picture composed of small pieces of colored glass, stone, or tile.

17. Nausea—a feeling of queasiness in the stomach that can lead to vomiting.

18. Ordination—the ceremony during which a man receives the Sacrament of Holy Orders. A man may be ordained a deacon, a priest, or a bishop.

19. Pediatrician—a doctor who specializes in the care of infants, children, and adolescents.

20. Italian Riviera—part of the Mediterranean coast called the Ligurian Sea that is very popular with tourists because of its beauty and warm climate.

21. Rosary—a prayer based on the Scriptures in which we think about important events in the lives of Jesus and Mary. The Rosary is made up of Our Fathers, Hail

Marys, and Glorys that we pray while using a circle of beads also called a rosary or rosary beads.

22. Third Order of St. Francis—a branch of the Franciscan Order for laypersons. Members make vows of poverty, chastity, and obedience, but they remain living at home following many spiritual practices of the Franciscan Order and observing a special rule of life. Today members of the Third Order are known as Secular Franciscans.

23. Triduum—a period of three days of prayer, which may come before a special feast or may prepare for an important event. The most well-known triduum is Holy Thursday, Good Friday, and Easter.

24. Tropics—a region of the Earth that is close to the equator and therefore very hot.

25. Vocation—a call from God to love and serve him in a particular state of life. A person may have a vocation to marriage, the priesthood, the religious life, or the single life. Everyone has a vocation to be holy.

26. Widower—a man whose wife has died.

St. Francis of Assisi

03147149

The Daughters of St. Paul operate book and media centers at the following addresses. Visit, call or write the one nearest you today, or find us on the World Wide Web, www.pauline.org

CALIFORNIA

```
282.09 WAL

Wallace, Susan Helen, 1940-
Saint Gianna Beretta Molla
: the gift of life.
```